EXPLORING OUR OCEANS

LIONFISH

SUSAN H. GRAY

Published in the United States of America by Cherry Lake Publishing
Ann Arbor, Michigan
www.cherrylakepublishing.com

Consultants: Dominique A. Didier, PhD, Associate Professor, Department of Biology, Millersville University;
Marla Conn, ReadAbility, Inc.
Book design: Sleeping Bear Press

Photo Credits: ©Cigdem Sean Cooper/Shutterstock Images, cover, 1, 29; ©Richard Whitcombe/Shutterstock Images, 5,
15, 16; ©Bildagentur Zoonar GmbH/Shutterstock Images, 6, 13; ©NORFANZ Founding Parties, 9; ©blueringmedia/
Thinkstock, 11; ©DaveLongMedia/iStock, 19; ©LauraD/Shutterstock Images, 21; ©orlandin/Shutterstock Images, 23;
©Rich Carey/Shutterstock Images, 25; ©Kristina Vackova/Shutterstock Images, 26; ©SFU Public Affairs and Media
Relations/http://www.flickr.com/ CC-BY-2.0, 27

Library of Congress Cataloging-in-Publication Data

Gray, Susan Heinrichs, author.
Lionfish / by Susan H. Gray.
    pages cm. — (Exploring our oceans)
    Summary: "Discover facts about lionfish, including physical features, habitat, life cycle, food,
and threats to these ocean creatures. Photos, captions, and keywords supplement the narrative of
this informational text— Provided by publisher.
    Audience: Age 8-12.
    Audience: Grades 4 to 6.
    Includes bibliographical references and index.
    ISBN 978-1-63188-019-3 (hardcover)—ISBN 978-1-63188-062-9 (pbk.)— ISBN 978-1-63188-105-3 (pdf)—
ISBN 978-1-63188-148-0 (ebook) 1. Pterois volitans—Juvenile literature. 2. Fishes—Juvenile literature. I. Title. II. Title:
Lionfish. III. Series: 21st century skills library. Exploring our oceans.

QL638.S42G73 2015
597.68—dc23   2014005348

Cherry Lake Publishing would like to acknowledge the work of
The Partnership for 21st Century Skills. Please visit www.p21.org
for more information.

Printed in the United States of America
Corporate Graphics Inc.

ABOUT THE AUTHOR

Susan H. Gray has a master's degree in zoology. She has worked in research and has taught
college-level science classes. Susan has also written more than 140 science and reference books, but
especially likes to write about animals. She and her husband, Michael, live in Cabot, Arkansas.

TABLE OF CONTENTS

CHAPTER 1
A New Life 4

CHAPTER 2
The Lionfish Body 8

CHAPTER 3
Meals for a Lionfish 14

CHAPTER 4
The Life of a Lionfish 20

CHAPTER 5
Beautiful and Troublesome ..24

THINK ABOUT IT 30
LEARN MORE 31
GLOSSARY 32
INDEX 32

A NEW LIFE

The hungry lionfish swam slowly along a rocky ledge. It was stalking a group of smaller fish for dinner. Spreading its fearsome **spines**, the lionfish backed three of the little fish into a corner. Nervously, they swam back and forth.

Suddenly, another animal appeared behind the lionfish. It was a huge grouper—one of the lionfish's few enemies. The lionfish turned to confront the danger. Now it was no longer concerned with eating. The three smaller fish saw their chance and shot away.

A lionfish hunts for food in the rocks.

Lionfish like to swim in warm water near the equator.

The lionfish is a native of the eastern Indian Ocean and the western Pacific. People in Japan, South Korea, and Malaysia have reported seeing the fish in nearby waters. People have also spotted it near Australia and New Zealand. The fish does not move too far north or south of the equator. It seems to prefer warmer seas.

In recent years, the lionfish has shown up in some new areas. It has appeared along the eastern coast of the United States. It has been seen in the Gulf of Mexico and near South America. Divers have spotted the lionfish near coral reefs, shipwrecks, and underwater bridge supports.

The fish is sometimes called the red lionfish because of its reddish stripes. People also call it the peacock lionfish and the turkey fish. This is because of the way the animal spreads its **pectoral** fins into large "fans."

GO DEEPER

FISH, CRABS, AND OTHER SEA CREATURES SEEM TO GATHER AROUND SHIPWRECKS. WHAT COULD BE SO ATTRACTIVE ABOUT A SHIPWRECK TO THESE SEA CREATURES?

THE LIONFISH BODY

The lionfish is a member of a large group of fish called the mail-cheeked fish. *Mail* is another word for "armor." These fish have bony ridges that run across their cheeks. Their skulls look like they are armored.

There are more than 1,000 different species, or kinds, of mail-cheeked fish. They are some of the most unusual fish in the sea. The tasseled scorpion fish is so warty, lumpy, and multicolored, it looks nothing like a fish. The lumpsucker has **adhesive** pads on its underside that help it cling to things. The red Indian fish has a **dorsal** fin

[21ST CENTURY SKILLS LIBRARY]

that runs from head to tail. And the blobfish, a distant relative of scorpion fish, is a weak swimmer. It usually just waits for food to drift by. Unlike the blobfish, the lionfish is no weakling. It is a fierce **predator** with few enemies.

Blobfish live in very deep waters off the coast of Australia.

Photo Credit © NORFANZ Founding Parties

Two of the most striking things about this fish are its stripes and its fins. From head to tail, the animal is covered in vertical stripes. These are deep red or brown against an off-white background.

Running down the lionfish's back is the dorsal fin. Just behind its head are the enormous pectoral fins. Farther back are the pelvic fins. A single anal fin is on the underside, near the tail. The fins are supported by stiff spines and slender, flexible **rays**. All of the fins, spines, and rays are spotted or striped.

Spines of the dorsal fin are quite tall and produce **venom**. The pelvic and anal fin spines are also venomous. Each spine comes to a sharply pointed tip. The tip is covered by a thin sleeve. Farther down the spine is the venom-producing tissue. When the spine's point pierces a victim, the sleeve is pushed back. This disturbs the venom-producing tissue, and venom is released. The venom of the lionfish is extremely toxic. The lionfish's sting can kill larger fish. People who are stung may feel pain and tingling for weeks.

BODY DIAGRAM

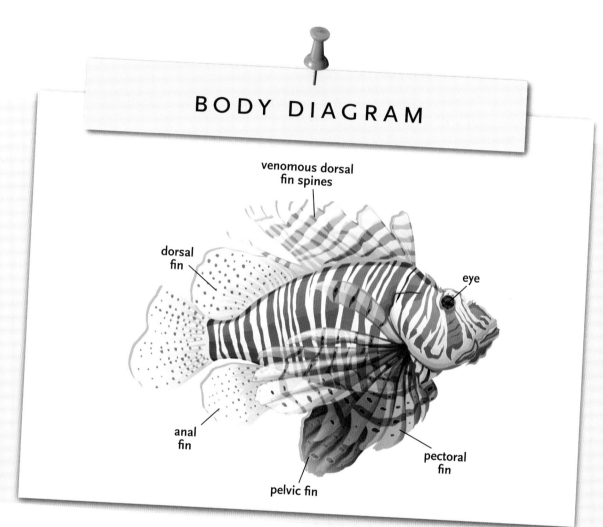

venomous dorsal
fin spines

dorsal
fin

eye

anal
fin

pectoral
fin

pelvic fin

The spines in the fins of a lionfish are venomous.

The eyes of the lionfish are difficult to see. This is because their black **pupils** are right in line with their dark stripes. Several fleshy tabs droop from the fish's lips and cheeks. In many lionfish, **tentacles** stick up just above the eyes. Even the tentacles and fleshy tabs are striped.

Lionfish have many small teeth in their jaws. A patch of teeth also lies in the roof of their mouth. The teeth are not for biting or chewing food. Scientists believe they are used for holding on to prey.

These fish never grow to a great size. Most adults reach lengths of only 12 to 15 inches (30.5 to 38.1 cm). Fully grown lionfish weigh just 2.6 pounds (1.2 kg). The lionfish may not be a big fish, but with all of its colors, patterns, spines, and fleshy face tabs, it looks quite frightening.

How do you think the lionfish got its name?

LOOK AGAIN

LOOK CLOSELY AT THIS PHOTOGRAPH. DOES IT
REMIND YOU OF ANOTHER ANIMAL?

MEALS FOR A LIONFISH

The lionfish is a **carnivorous** predator. It hunts and eats all sorts of other animals. Scientists have opened up the stomachs of dead lionfish to see what's inside. They have found shrimp, crabs, octopuses, and small fish. They have discovered that lionfish will even eat members of their own species.

When it's not eating, the lionfish often retreats to a protected spot. This might be a shadowy place with crevices and rocky ledges. There, it hovers quietly in the water, often with its head pointed down.

This lionfish gets a mouthful of small silverside baitfish for dinner.

Lionfish use their wide fins to confuse prey.

When the lionfish is hungry, it springs into action. It becomes a fierce hunter. Once it spies a small prey fish, it spreads its pectoral fins. Such a display confuses an unsuspecting fish, which then moves away. The lionfish follows and soon has its prey cornered. There is nowhere for the prey to go. In an instant, the lionfish sucks the little fish right into its mouth. It swallows the prey whole.

The stomach of the lionfish is an extremely stretchy organ. In fact, it can stretch to 30 times its normal size. This enables the animal to devour an enormous amount of food. It also allows the fish to go for long periods without eating. Scientists report that lionfish have gone as long as three months without a meal.

The lionfish certainly has some excellent survival tactics. It can **ambush** and corner its prey. It can wipe out dozens of small animals in one feeding. It can go without eating for weeks. It can inflict intense pain on an enemy. These abilities are great for the lionfish's survival. But they do nothing to help anything else in the environment. In fact, these traits cause many problems.

Lionfish often live on or near coral reefs. On the reefs, there are all sorts of fish, crabs, sea slugs, anemones, and plants. The plants grow in the sunlight. Some animals eat the plants, and some eat other animals. No single species takes over. Things stay in balance.

Problems occur when new species are introduced. They may have no natural enemies. They might wipe out some of the fish that keep plants on the coral reef under control. These new species upset the balance of the reef **ecosystem**.

This is what is happening with the lionfish in the Gulf of Mexico. It is happening along the eastern coast of the United States. It is also occurring in the Caribbean. The lionfish has invaded the area, and it is eating everything it can.

How did the lionfish get there? It probably happened when people released their pet lionfish into the ocean. In 1985, scientists first heard of a lionfish near the Florida coast. By 2000, lionfish had been seen near Georgia, South Carolina, and North Carolina. Now, reports of the fish are coming from New York, the Caribbean, and South America.

Clams can live in the same habitat as lionfish.

LOOK AGAIN

LOOK CLOSELY AT THIS PHOTOGRAPH OF CLAMS. LIONFISH EAT LOTS OF THINGS. DO YOU THINK THEY COULD EAT CLAMS? WHY OR WHY NOT?

THE LIFE OF A LIONFISH

Lionfish begin their lives in egg masses. These are clumps of several thousand eggs held together by a jellylike material. The egg masses float at the water's surface. After a few days, the jelly breaks down and the eggs drift apart. The baby lionfish hatch and float freely.

Not much is known about this stage of the fish's life. But scientists believe that the babies are smaller than pinheads when they hatch. They probably are free-floating for around 25 to 40 days. During this time, they eat other free-floating animals that are extremely small.

As a larva, the lionfish has a big head and a few spines. It also has just a bit of the adult's coloring. Some colors appear on its pectoral fins and near the tail. As the larva grows, its spines, fins, and colors become more obvious.

This baby lionfish is already much larger than it was when it hatched.

In time, the young fish begins to eat larger and larger prey. Its digestive system lengthens, and its little stomach is able to expand more.

It takes a year or two before the lionfish becomes an adult. Then it is time for it to have babies of its own. Usually, lionfish live alone and do not travel in schools. But during **courtship**, things are different. Males and females get together in the evening hours. While courting, they circle, follow, and lead one another well past dark.

Finally, the female releases masses of eggs into the water. The male then releases **sperm** cells in the same area. The egg and sperm cells unite, forming tiny new lionfish. Thousands of babies are clumped together in the egg mass. Soon, the mass rises slowly to the surface.

Lionfish can go through this process all year long. They do not have to wait until the weather or the season is right. As a result, lionfish can produce thousands of young month after month.

Many types of fish like to travel in schools. Why do you think a group of fish is called a school?

LOOK AGAIN

LOOK CLOSELY AT THIS PHOTOGRAPH SHOWING A SCHOOL OF FISH. WHY DO SOME FISH LIKE THESE TRAVEL IN SCHOOLS? WHY DON'T THE LIONFISH NEED TO TRAVEL AS A GROUP?

BEAUTIFUL AND TROUBLESOME

The lionfish seems to have no enemies at all. It can eat just about any fish, as long as it is small enough. It threatens larger fish with its venomous spines. It is taking over reef communities in the western Atlantic. Can anything get this fish under control?

Scientists are working on this problem. They have found that some fish actually do eat the lionfish. Groupers are known to devour them. They actually swallow the lionfish tail-first. This way, they avoid the stinging spines. Unfortunately, there are not enough groupers to make a dent in the lionfish population.

Groupers, like this one, will eat lionfish tail-first!

Experts are rapidly gathering information on the lionfish. They need to know how quickly and how far the fish have spread. This tells them which new areas need protection. Divers, sport fishers, students, and others are helping to gather data. They report when and where they have seen lionfish.

In many places, there are too many lionfish for the ecosystem to support.

Why do you think it is important for people to help balance the lionfish population?

The public has also gotten involved in other ways. For example, businesspeople have come up with programs to control the fish. Marine sanctuary staff and dive shop owners are teaching divers how to spear lionfish. Divers learn how to do this without damaging the reefs. Restaurant owners are putting lionfish on their menus. And cities are holding lionfishing tournaments. These efforts help to draw attention to the lionfish. But they are not likely to solve the problem. The fish still produce young by the thousands.

Fortunately, not all of the lionfish news is bad. Researchers have been studying its venom. They think it might slow the growth of cancer cells. If this is the case, lionfish might help to cure cancer patients.

The lionfish is truly a remarkable animal. Its color patterns are stunning. It has quite effective feeding habits. It has an amazing defense system. And its venom may have healing properties. We still have much to learn about this beautiful yet troublesome fish.

THINK ABOUT IT

SUPPOSE SOMEONE BROUGHT IN MILLIONS OF GROUPER TO EAT THE LIONFISH. WOULD THIS BE A GOOD WAY TO SOLVE THE LIONFISH PROBLEM? WHY OR WHY NOT?

The venom in the spines of a lionfish may help to treat cancer and other diseases.

THINK ABOUT IT

- Clearly, releasing pets into the wild is not a good idea. So what should aquarium owners do if they can no longer keep their lionfish?

- Other fish, such as the butterfly fish, have eyes that are hidden by stripes. What might be an advantage to this feature?

- Sometimes, Florida gets hit by hurricanes. Could a hurricane have caused pet lionfish to wind up in the ocean?

- In chapter 2 we learned that lionfish produce venom. So how can they be safe for people to eat?

LEARN MORE

FURTHER READING

Bagai, Shona. *Designed to Survive: All About Fins*. New Delhi, India: The Energy and Resources Institute, 2011.

Berger, Gilda, and Berger, Melvin. *101 Freaky Animals*. Danbury, CT: Scholastic, 2010.

Niver, Heather. *20 Fun Facts about Lionfish*. New York: Gareth Stevens Publishing, 2012.

WEB SITES

A–Z Animals—Lionfish
http://a-z-animals.com/animals/lionfish
Visit this Web site to view several photos of lionfish and lionfish information, including the fish's scientific classification.

National Geographic—Lionfish
http://animals.nationalgeographic.com/animals/fish/lionfish
Read additional facts about lionfish and look at a map showing where the lionfish live.

GLOSSARY

adhesive (ad-HEE-siv) tending to stick together

ambush (AM-bush) an attack done by waiting or hiding rather than by using speed or strength

carnivorous (kahr-NIV-uh-russ) eating other animals

courtship (KOHRT-ship) specialized behavior that leads to mating

dorsal (DOR-suhl) on or toward the back of an animal

ecosystem (EE-koh-sis-tuhm) a system that involves all of the interactions between living things and their environment

pectoral (PEK-tur-ul) on, near to, or relating to the chest

predator (PRED-uh-tur) an animal that hunts and eats other animals

pupils (PYOO-puhlz) the openings in the iris of the eyes that allow in light

rays (RAYZ) flexible rods that support the fins of many fish

sperm (SPURM) male reproductive cell

spines (SPINEZ) stiff rods that support the fins of many fish

tentacles (TEN-tuh-kuhlz) slender, flexible limbs or appendages in an animal, used for grasping or moving around, or containing sense organs

venom (VEN-uhm) a poisonous fluid that some animals secrete and inject into their prey

INDEX

babies, 20, 22
body, 8–13

cancer, 28
color, 7, 10, 21, 28

eggs, 20, 22
enemies, 24

fins, 7, 10, 11, 16
food, 5, 14–19

habitat, 6–7, 13

larvae, 21
life cycle, 20–23

mail-cheeked fish, 8

poison, 10
predators/prey, 4, 9, 12, 14, 16, 22, 24–25
problems, 17–18, 24–27

schools, 22, 23
size, 12
spines, 4, 10, 11, 24
stomach, 17
stripes, 10, 12

venom, 10, 11, 24, 28–29